Facts About the African Wild Dog

By Lisa Strattin

© 2019 Lisa Strattin

FREE BOOK

FREE FOR ALL SUBSCRIBERS

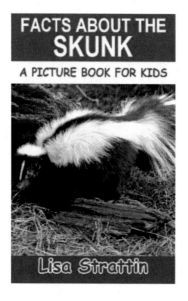

LisaStrattin.com/Subscribe-Here

BOX SET

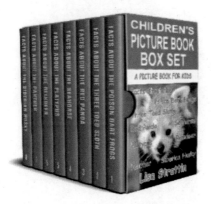

- **FACTS ABOUT THE POISON DART FROGS**
- **FACTS ABOUT THE THREE TOED SLOTH**
- **FACTS ABOUT THE RED PANDA**
- **FACTS ABOUT THE SEAHORSE**
- **FACTS ABOUT THE PLATYPUS**
- **FACTS ABOUT THE REINDEER**
- **FACTS ABOUT THE PANTHER**
- **FACTS ABOUT THE SIBERIAN HUSKY**

LisaStrattin.com/BookBundle

Facts for Kids Picture Books by Lisa Strattin

Little Blue Penguin, Vol 92

Chipmunk, Vol 5

Frilled Lizard, Vol 39

Blue and Gold Macaw, Vol 13

Poison Dart Frogs, Vol 50

Blue Tarantula, Vol 115

African Elephants, Vol 8

Amur Leopard, Vol 89

Sabre Tooth Tiger, Vol 167

Baboon, Vol 174

Sign Up for New Release Emails Here

LisaStrattin.com/subscribe-here

COVER IMAGE

https://www.flickr.com/photos/berniedup/6017661441/

ADDITIONAL IMAGES

https://www.flickr.com/photos/arnolouise/5070787743/

https://www.flickr.com/photos/mathiasappel/33545653736/

https://www.flickr.com/photos/arnolouise/3621583860/

https://www.flickr.com/photos/arnolouise/4207599965/

https://www.flickr.com/photos/mathiasappel/32622720206/

https://www.flickr.com/photos/110394983@N04/15103097325/

https://www.flickr.com/photos/55031801@N02/6352074296/

https://www.flickr.com/photos/arnolouise/3659047775/

https://www.flickr.com/photos/arnolouise/5220476647/

https://www.flickr.com/photos/mathiasappel/31027637745/

Contents

INTRODUCTION... 9

BEHAVIOR... 11

APPEARANCE 13

REPRODUCTION... 15

LIFE SPAN 17

SIZE 19

HABITAT.. 21

DIET 23

ENEMIES.. 25

SUITABILITY AS PETS..................................... 27

INTRODUCTION

The African Wild Dog is also called the Painted Dog. As a matter of fact, their name in Latin means "Painted Wolf."

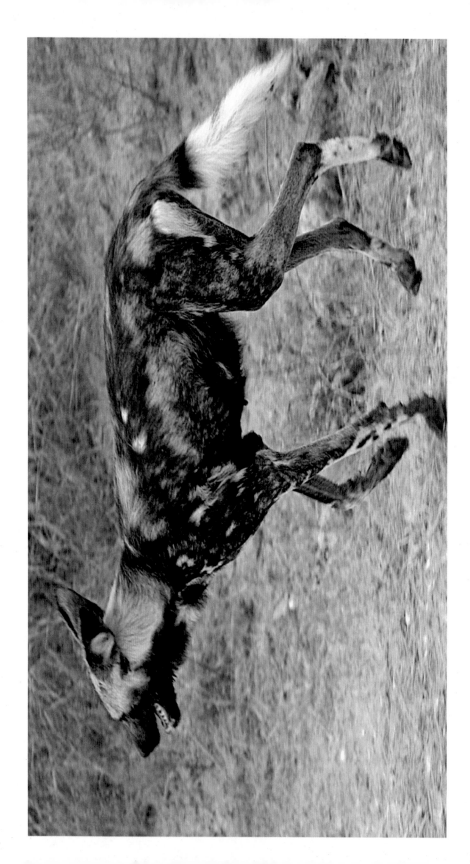

BEHAVIOR

African Wild Dogs are very social and usually get together in groups, known as packs, with 10 to 30 individual dogs. The leaders of the pack are always the dominant male and female breeding pair. They do everything together as a group, whether it involved taking care of the sick members to hunting and sharing the food they find. They are very good friends with one another in the pack. They have been observed licking each other and even wagging their tails when they are together as a group.

APPEARANCE

The African Wild Dog has mottled fur, which is just another way of saying it has patches of color all over. Colors can be red, white, brown, tan, black and yellow, with all colors obvious on an animal in patterns These colors act as camouflage to help the dog blend into their surroundings. They have very large ears, especially when you compare them to the average house pet. They have really long legs and a long muzzle. They only have four toes on each foot, unlike the dog we have as pets that have five toes on each foot.

REPRODUCTION

In the African Wild Dog pack, there is normally one breeding pair. The female is pregnant for just over two months and will have a litter of between 2 and 20 pups. The mother stays with the pups in her den for the first couple of weeks, while other dogs from the pack will bring her food to eat. The pups are able to leave the mother's den when they are about 2 to 3 months old, but they are still taken care of by the other members of the pack until they can leave to go out on their own. Sometimes they leave to join another pack, other times, they will go start a new pack of their own.

LIFE SPAN

The average lifespan of an African Wild Dog is 10 to 13 years.

SIZE

Adult African Wild Dogs are usually about 2 to 3.5 feet long and weigh as much as 80 pounds.

HABITAT

The African Wild Dog lives in the deserts, savannas and plains of sub-Saharan Africa. Today, they are mostly restricted to the National Parks that have been established across Africa. There are currently more of them found in the countries of Botswana and Zimbabwe than in other areas of Africa.

DIET

The African Wild Dog is a meat-eater and will eat pretty much whatever crosses their path. They will go after large animals like Antelope and Warthogs, but also, lizards, birds, rodents and insects. They have been known to go after animals as large as the Wildebeest!

ENEMIES

There are not many natural enemies in the native range that the African Wild Dog must worry about. Although lions and hyenas have been known to hunt the ones that get separated from the pack, most animals are prey for them, not predator.

SUITABILITY AS PETS

The African Wild Dog is not suitable to be a pet. They need a lot of meat and, by nature, want to hunt and chase their prey.

There are zoos that have some of these Dogs in habitats where you could see them, and that is probably the best idea if you want to watch some up close.

COLOR ME

COLOR ME

COLOR ME

COLOR ME

COLOR ME

COLOR ME

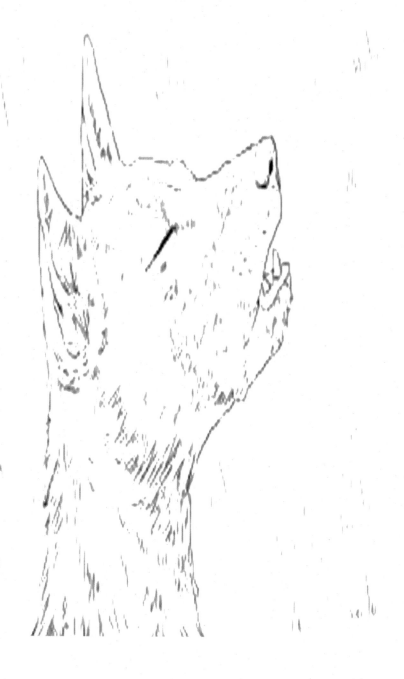

COLOR ME

COLOR ME

COLOR ME

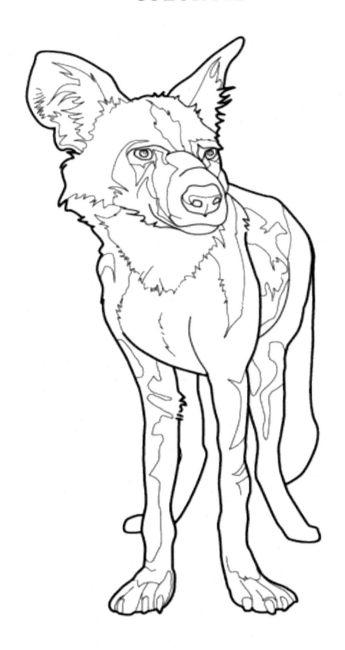

Please leave me a review here:

LisaStrattin.com/Review-Vol-344

For more Kindle Downloads Visit Lisa Strattin Author Page on Amazon Author Central

amazon.com/author/lisastrattin

To see upcoming titles, visit my website at LisaStrattin.com– most books available on Kindle!

LisaStrattin.com

FREE BOOK

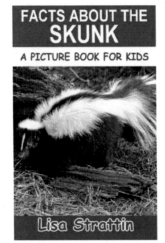

Made in the USA
Las Vegas, NV
13 October 2024

96770904R00026